POCKET WISDOM
— FOR —
SPEAKERS

How To Captivate And Connect With Your Audience

I0465933

BOB 'IDEA MAN' HOOEY, ACCREDITED SPEAKER
AUTHOR OF SPEAKING FOR SUCCESS

Take charge of your fears and learn to be a powerful presenter.

1

A word as we begin,

Why would 'YOU' want to invest time to improve your speaking and presentation skills? Perhaps the answers to these questions might give you some insight.

Are you interested in **learning a new skill** that will make a 'major' difference in your career and long-term business success?

Would you like to be **more productive** in your work and more profitable in your sales and marketing efforts?

Are you interested in acquiring a new skill that will develop your abilities to **effectively work with other people** and foster an enhanced sense of positive team?

Are you interested in changing or **enhancing your leadership** or career?

Would you like to learn an interviewing technique to give you a **definitive edge on your competition**?

Do you want to **feel more comfortable** while presenting in public?

If so, **read on fellow traveler** on the path of applied learning! Your increased self-confidence will 'filter' through to other areas in your professional life and actions. I've seen this happen with students at various colleges where I taught and repeatedly with my executive coaching clients.

This version of Pocket Wisdom for Speakers was originally designed to fit in your pocket. Along the way we've updated it and now offer it on-line in an e-pub format in addition to the original pocket format. Visit www.SuccessPublications.ca for more information or order on-line at Amazon.

I've shared these ideas with senior executives from some of Canada's 50 Best Managed Companies as well as leaders around the globe. I've seen this demonstrated even more dramatically when coaching on a one-to-one basis or in small group settings. Mastering this success skill may well be a 'pivotal' point in your career.

Why do some people succeed in advancing their careers while others do not? About 20 years ago, AT&T commissioned Stanford University to conduct a survey to see if there were any reliable indicators of their success.

Surprisingly, their results revealed *"The top predictors of success and upward mobility, professionally, were how much you enjoy public speaking and how effective you are!"*

Based on my management and leadership experience over the past 29 plus years, their survey result was not a big surprise. People who become proficient at something that most of us fear are bound to be noticed!

According to the 'Book of Lists', the #1 fear for most of us is speaking in public. The old joke, **"Most people are so afraid of giving a speech they'd rather be in the casket than giving the eulogy!"** certainly applies.

Best-selling author, and successful speaker, **Peter Drucker** wisely fore-cast, **"As soon as you move one step up from the bottom, your effectiveness depends on your ability to reach others through the spoken or written word."**

My core focus for creating **Pocket Wisdom for Speakers** is to share basic guidelines that will help you to improve your presentation skills and help position you to succeed in your chosen field of endeavor. It will take work on your part, but it is well worth your effort!

No success skill is ever acquired without concentrated and continuous effort on the part of the student. It can also be fun! It can be a richly rewarding journey, one that you will pause and reflect upon in years to come. You'll look back and see significant changes you've made in your life, career, and your personal effectiveness.

Your ability to speak in front of audiences will improve in direct proportion to the amount of time you dedicate to prepare and practice your skills. These speaking success skills are learned, not just from a book, but from your 'real life' experience in front of an audience.

Whether your desire is to simply overcome your fear of standing and delivering a presentation in front of an audience or stepping onto the stage as a paid professional speaker, these tips and techniques will form the foundation to see you desires fulfilled.

I've learned the hardest part of my job as a professional speaker is the work I do 'before' I walk on stage. Once I've done my homework, I simply share my stories and messages.

It gets easier as I apply my skills and refine my focus by making sure that what I share is of value for my audiences.

Bob 'Idea Man' Hooey
Accredited Speaker

"Your ability to communicate with others will account for fully 85% of your success in your business and in your life."
Brian Tracy

Where can I apply these new skills?

You may encounter some opportunities to give specialized presentations. The basics taught in the rest of this little manual will certainly apply in each of these examples.

You need to be aware of these different types of speeches and realize their objectives determine and influence their format.

- **Introductions:** You might be called on to introduce a speaker, facilitator, or trainer.
- **Welcome presentations:** You might be called on to say a few words if a group visits your workplace.
- **Acceptance speeches:** Imagine you've just been honored or given an award.
- **Inauguration speech:** You've just been elected to a leadership role in a volunteer group and called on to say a few words following the election.
- **Eulogies:** an emotionally challenging role, if you were close to the person who has recently passed away and are called to say a few words about their life.
- **New employee orientations:** While part of the opening management team for the first two BC Home Depots, we used to take turns doing this for new hires to outline what we expected of them and to help them settle into our culture.
- **A farewell speech:** Stepping down from a leadership role or leaving a long-term position in a company or group, you might want to say a few words of thanks and reflect on the time you spent and the people who touched or enriched your life.

Each of these unique situations has a different focus and purpose and would be structured and delivered appropriately.

If presented with the opportunity of doing one of these, take a minute to decide what you want to accomplish. Give some thought on how to best structure it to effectively reach that goal or objective.

Treat each as an opportunity to practice and polish your skills. Treat each as an opportunity to expand your toolbox of experience in front of an audience.

Moving upward

"the top predictor of success and upward mobility, professionally, is how much you enjoy public speaking and how effective you are at it!"
Stanford University Survey for AT&T

"As soon as you move one step up from the bottom, your effectiveness depends on your ability to reach others through the spoken or written word."
Peter Drucker, Best Selling Leadership Author

"Effective speaking skills are an essential foundation for success in any endeavor. Professionally or personally, it is one of the most important skills you'll ever acquire! And they are easily acquired!"
Bob 'Idea Man' Hooey, DTM, PDG, Accredited Speaker

Touching on the basics...

The cardinal rule to being truly effective in public speaking is **"NEVER BE BORING!"** But, how do we do this when we are nervous and under stress to perform?

Over the past 15 years, I've been teaching my clients and classes that the **"three keys to speaking success"** are based on acquiring the knowledge you need to successfully capture their attention, connect with your audience, and achieve your shared objectives.

Those three keys are simply:

- **KNOW** your subject or topic
- **KNOW** your audience
- **KNOW** yourself

If you **know your subject** and are thoroughly prepared, you will be much more relaxed than if you are 'winging' it. Taking time to organize and delve into your topic will give you a sense of the depth you bring to the platform or situation. It will also give you much more information for additional presentations and questions.

This confidence, based on acquired knowledge, works wonders in helping to keep the "butterflies flying in formation".

If you **know your audience**, you are better prepared to effectively analyze their needs and select from the body of knowledge you've acquired on your topic to serve or solve those needs.

The better you know their backgrounds, connections, education, gender, and their ages; the better you will be able to construct and deliver your presentation in a way that is interesting and informative to them.

If you **know yourself**, you can draw on your own experiences, and build on your own strengths in developing your own speaking style. You can also share your own unique stories in a way that allows you to be your most effective.

Self- knowledge is a tool of effective communication. Continually ask yourself, **"If I was in the audience, 'why' would I be interested in this point or topic?"** Then, simply make sure you have fully researched a good answer for that question.

Your audiences are people, just like you.

The better you know yourself, the better equipped you are to effectively reach them.

By combining your knowledge of self, your subject, and your audience, you will effectively increase your impact. You will also expand your impact as a presenter, interviewee, or speaker.

PRACTICE, PRACTICE, PRACTICE!

There is no substitute for being prepared; practicing until you are certain you are ready to present your material in a confident manner.

Using Humor – a few tips

People like to have fun and, in most countries I've visited, love to laugh with you. Creating places for natural humor in your presentations allow them to enjoy their time with you.

If you are going to use humor, more specifically jokes, **keep these tips in mind.**

Punch lines? Remember them!!!!

Ensure the anecdote is appropriate and relates to your presentation – and not inserted just for the laughs

Timing is everything – practice a lot!!!

BE KIND! Don't pick on any group or person. Pick on yourself!

Vulgarity and sexist remarks are NOT allowed. They work against you.

Humor doesn't travel well. Make sure it works in different locations.

"We all have a life story and a message that can inspire others to live a better life or run a better business. Why not use that story and message to serve others and grow a real business doing it?"
Brendon Burchard

Foundations for Success

These success 'foundations' will work for you! The knowledge gleaned from their wisdom is the secret to being able to walk confidently up to the front and deliver a message that means something to your audiences.

The secret in making sure the audience gets the best presentation possible, with the most value, blended with personal stories and teaching points, is in the preparation.

Questions…thoughtful questions can be the keys that unlock the door to success in any venture. This is no less true if your desire is to be a confident speaker, who connects with their audience, and leaves them wanting more.

WHY are you speaking?

WHAT do you want to accomplish?

WHO is your audience?

WHEN will you be speaking?

HOW long will you be speaking?

WHERE will you be speaking?

WHAT tools will you use? (ie. PPT, flip charts)

Knowing the answers to these questions helps in your preparation and in crafting an engaging talk.

Getting a hand up

One exercise I share with my students is to ask them to hold up and look at their hand. "What do you see?" I ask them. They normally say, "A thumb and 4 fingers." Which, of course, is the obvious answer.

My answer to that same question is "A talk or presentation, up to 20 minutes, without notes." I see an opening, 3 points, and a conclusion.

I can remember 5 Things! Can't you? When we keep it simple and focus on the main points it makes it easier for us to remember.

The Opening (Thumb) is telling them what you're going to tell them, the central theme or objective for your presentation.

The Three Points (middle fingers) illustrate, expand, develop, or support that theme. Simply telling them. I cover the 1st point and then move on to each successive one. Depending on the time, your points can be expanded or contracted, by adding additional stories, examples or illustrations.

The conclusion (little finger) reminds them of the central theme, summaries the 3 points, and of course, tells them what you've just told them.

When speaking, extra attention needs to be given to crafting both your openings and conclusions. People will often only remember your opening statement or something you've said in closing.

Accepting this trend in audience behaviour as accurate, work a little harder on your opening and closing, to ensure they are tight and create vivid pictures in your audience's mind.

As an audience member, you have about 30 seconds to capture my attention and draw me into the subject of your presentation.

Choose your words carefully.

Avoid weak or timid openings with trite questions like: *"Do you ever wonder…?" "How many of you have…?"* (These have been way overdone.)

Avoid a slow moving, lengthy statement or story that doesn't relate to your subject.

Avoid an apologetic statement or excuse such as *"I wasn't ready, but…"* Never build a case against yourself or tell me (audience) you're not prepared…. let me find out for myself! (smile) Telling me you aren't prepared says, *"I'm not important enough for you to do your homework and prepare in advance to meet my needs."* It insults the audience.

Don't open with a joke or humorous story unless you have it down cold and it is relevant to the audience and your presentation.

Don't waste the audience's time with thank yous and general opening remarks. Get into the meat of your presentation and grab my mind and my heart! Having said that, it is important to acknowledge the person who introduced you and the audience.

I see this overdone and it weakens your opening impact. Save it for a bit later, after you have me more engaged! You don't have to open with them.

All about them...

Issue of some concern
(You're concerned ... I understand)

Point of view
*(This is a different point of view ...
of looking at your problem)*

Support
(Here is how it will work for you ... the evidence)

Resolution (plan, proposal, idea)
(Here is the idea ... with benefits for you)

Next Step
(Here is your next step...)

*Successful speakers keep their focus
on the audience*

Good openings make or break your presentation to establish connection with your audience. I remember learning about openings when I joined Toastmasters.

As I recall, **good openings incorporate various elements:**
- Tend to be short, punchy and dramatic or thought provoking.

- Contain a startling statement, position, intrigue, or a challenging question.
- An appropriate and relevant quotation, story excerpts, ironies, paradoxes, idiosyncrasies, good and bad experiences, or a personal story or illustration.
- A general or universal statement that ties in or relates to your subject, while acting as an attention getter to draw them into your presentation.
- Visuals, a display, or an appropriate or relevant prop or picture.
- References to a shared or common experience with your audience.
- Drawn from life, based on journalized stories, reading, listening to stories, and conversations with others.

Keeping our attention is a challenge. People can listen at 400-500 words per minute while we normally talk at 125-175 words per minute. This gap needs to be handled in the development of your presentation. We'll explore more about how to do that in the development of the body of your remarks and how to keep your audience involved.

Remember to create word pictures for our minds. If you don't, we tend to think about other areas. We think about grocery lists, work undone, or even fantasize about sex, when we are not involved mentally. Similarly, creating captivating closings are critical to our speaking success.

Effective closings incorporate certain key elements:
- Summarize your major speech points and the conclusion or actions to be drawn from them.
- Bring them back to the main theme or purpose of your presentation.

- A relevant story, illustration, or quotation that re-emphasizes the major point or central theme of your presentation.

I attended a presentation skills lab in Phoenix, AZ hosted by the NSA. One of our instructors, **Mark Sanborn, CSP**, asked us some questions that are worth considering.

- Are your closings a culmination or a stopping point for your talk?
- What one thing could you do to make your presentation more of an experience? (Hint: Esthetics, escapism, education, and entertainment?)
- What impression are you trying to leave after your speech? Why?
- What are the 2-3 most important values that drive your life? Do they show up in your presentations? How?

And, isn't that what you really want?

Mark talked about timing, too. **FEAR - false endings appearing real.**

Have you ever been listening to a speaker and thought they were closing, only to find they still had lots 'more' to say? How did you feel? Don't do that to your audiences. When it's time to close, do so and do it with impact. Go for the close and finish on time.

Use gestures to channel your nervous muscle tension by carefully selecting or choreographing body movements that emphasize specific speech points. Nervous energy can be used effectively to lend welcome animation to your movements and presentation.

Audiences believe what they see in your face, manners, and body movement long BEFORE they believe what you say.

Gestures amplify your speech by including facial expressions and body language to illustrate pain, pleasure, sarcasm, sincerity, enthusiasm or disinterest, and other emotions.

Smooth, natural gestures or body movements will add to the effectiveness of your presentation. They enrich, extend, emphasize, or clarify your message. They also help define size, shape, location, direction, or weight.

Gestures can denote relative importance or urgency and assist in outlining contrasts or comparisons. They should be large enough to be seen, but not exaggerated as to distract from your message.

Make sure the message sent to the EARS of your audience correlates and is supported by the VISUAL one received by them.

"Picture yourself in a living room having a chat with your friends. You would be relaxed and comfortable talking to them, the same applies when public speaking."
Richard Branson

Handling nervousness...

Don't fight it!

Take a brisk walk.

Don't sit with your legs crossed.

**Let your arms dangle at your sides
while you're sitting waiting to speak.**

**While your arms are dangling, twirl your wrists
so your fingers shake loosely.**

**Pretend you're wearing an overcoat
and you can feel it resting on your shoulders.**

**Waggle your jaw back and forth
three or four times.**

Deep breathing.

Say to yourself, "Let go!"

**Don't be self conscious about having
a warm up routine.**

The biggest secret to being confident and not allowing your normal nervousness to affect your presentation – do your homework! And, make sure you have invested the time to practice and prepare for each audience.

A 12-step process
(for building a winning presentation)

This guideline is almost self-explanatory in preparing for a presentation. The core secret in outlining an effective presentation is in being systematic and building toward your goal.

Use this 12 Step format or use the examples from the following pages as creative methods to gather your thoughts and organize them in a relevant and orderly manner.

Then, deliver them with passion and persuade your audience to accept and act on them.

1. **Select the Topic**
2. **Limit the Topic to One Central Theme (what is the most important goal)**
3. **Gather the Information**
4. **Choose a Method of Organization**
5. **Outline Your Main Points**
6. **Collect Supporting Data**
7. **Check for Accuracy**
8. **Design the Introduction**
9. **Write a Strong Conclusion**
10. **Put Together a Final Draft**
11. **Practice Your Presentation**
12. **Practice, Practice, Practice**

Following this simple 12-step process will help you take the journey from idea to implementation in front of an audience.

It works well because it is systematic. This format works for a variety of presentation styles and situations.

You'll find two additional templates to use in blocking out your speech. One is the more linear model and the second a mind mapping format that has proven invaluable in allowing me to adapt and change my presentations on-site.

In each case, your starting point is distilling your main message to a sentence or at the most two. This creates a focus for your work in creating the presentation itself.

Bob delivering a speech on effective leadership

When I create a presentation, I craft a rough opening format which is refined once I have outlined the 3 main points, any stories, or examples. I then carefully craft my summary to close.

Speech Crafting—Traditional linear outline model

Main Message

Opening

1st Point

2nd Point

3rd Point

Close

This is along the lines of how we organize our thoughts to write something. It can work with presenting, but is not as flexible.

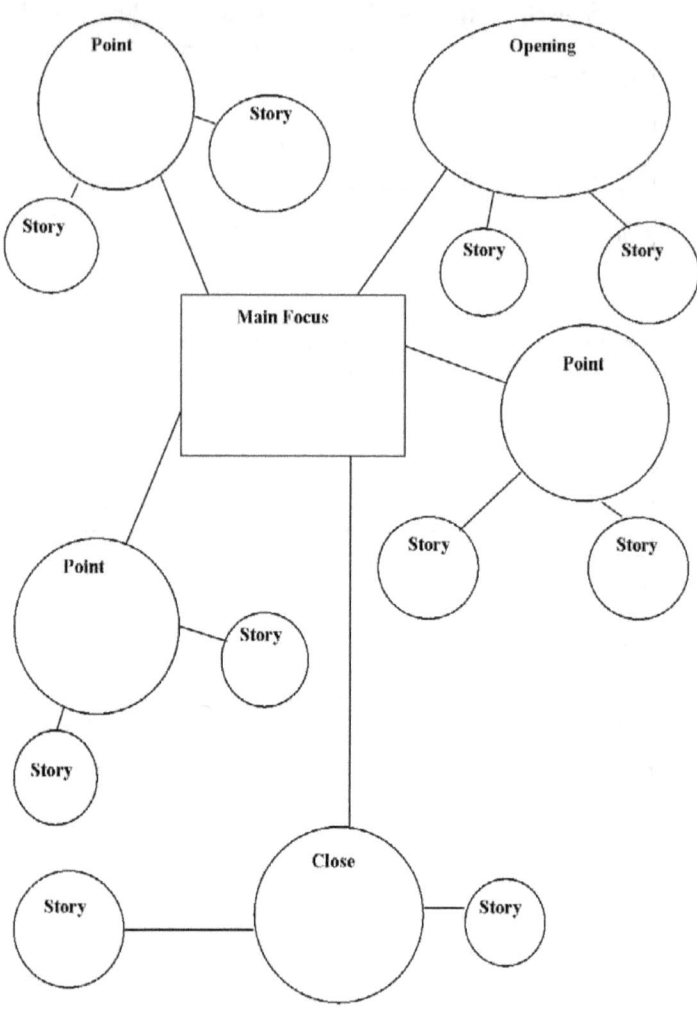

Mind Mapping Sample Speech Outline

This is more like how we think. Easier to organize.
Capture your thoughts, make the connection, re-organize
and deliver.

Use contents from your **"Spice Cupboard"** to add additional interest to your talk. This helps you capture and connect with your audience.

Stories – that convey emotion and grab their attention as well as encapsulate the lessons. Make sure to use your own stories as they have more impact. If you share from another source, make sure you give proper credits.

Quotes – that reinforce or remind them of your message.

Facts – to substantiate or reinforce your credibility on the platform.

Props – that help illustrate or command attention.

Costumes – use them if they enhance your presentation and illustrate your point.

Handouts/learning guides – that give sold value and follow up information on a part of the presentation.

Audio – sound bites and background music to assist in lesson or setting moods.

Video – illustrate a point, introduce another concept or expert into the mix.

"The single most important skill you must have to lead is the ability to tell your own story."
Bo Eason

Your VOICE is a Powerful Communications Tool!

Your voice can be the most powerful tool in your communications by conveying information, meaning, emotion, and enthusiasm for your subject. Or it can work against you; to make it hard for your audience to grasp what you are trying to say. Use it to your best advantage.

I learned early in my speaking journey that to be a good speaker there are five basic characteristics of a good speaking voice.
- A **pleasant tone**, which can convey a sense of warmth and friendliness.
- A **vitality**, which lends the impression of force, strength, and conviction.
- A **natural sound** that reflects and echoes your sincerity and true personality.
- **Portraying various shades of meaning** to minimize monotony or lack of emotion.
- **Easily heard**: learn and apply proper volume, projection, and ar-tic-u-lation.

The objective of a good speaking voice is to find, develop, and maintain a balance between the extremes of volume, pitch, and rate, while seeking to find and deliver a pleasing sound quality. It sounds difficult, but it simply requires awareness and application of some basic principles. Perhaps a little coaching wouldn't hurt either.

Volume: can be varied to add emphasis or dramatic impact. Make sure everyone can hear you. Don't overpower your audience.

24

Pitch: can be varied to convey emotion and conviction. Avoid a too high pitch; this can suggest excitability or reveal your nervousness. These take away from your strength and credibility as a presenter. Make a conscious effort to be conversational in your speaking. Focus on making it easy for your audience to hear and listen to you.

Rate: maintain a rate of 125-160 words per minute, which seems to be the most effective speaking rate. Vary your rate during your presentation to create emphasis and reflect mood changes. Slow down when you want the audience to listen carefully or emphasize an important point. Speed up to convey urgency or excitement in the moment.

Quality: relax your throat while you speak for increased vocal quality. Do a warm up before you begin to speak to allow your throat and muscles to prepare to deliver their best for you. *(I sometimes do it in the washroom before I am scheduled to speak.)* Think in terms of friendliness, confidence, and a desire to communicate clearly with your audience.

Tone: work to mold your tone; friendly and pleasant, not harsh and monotonous. Your audience will appreciate it and stay tuned to hear what you are saying.

Vitality: work on making your voice forceful and expressive when appropriate in your presentation and consistent with what you really feel.

Ar-tic-u-lation: If they don't hear you clearly, your message may be lost. Work to be clear and distinct. Don't drop the hard letters like 'g' at the end of words.

Learn and apply the proper pronunciations for words. Don't let your critical message be misunderstood just because your words are misunderstood.

In business, we have 500 more commonly used words with close to 5000 connotations. The wide range of connotations depend on how they are used and pronounced. Be clear, let us hear, and understand you!

A few more suggestions and comments:

- Practice using warm up exercises to give your voice its optimum range and to give your audience the best message possible.
- Make sure you drink lots of water – room temperature water with no ice before you speak. Don't be afraid to have water close at hand or to stop and take a sip from time to time while speaking. It's also a nice way to take a break and collect your thoughts. A slice of lemon can be added to your water.
- Drinking ice water can be tough on your throat, as it tends to shrink or cause your muscles to contract. Remember the last time you had a sprain and had an ice pack. Don't do that to your throat, especially at a time when it is already under stress.
- Take a moment to breathe and ground yourself prior to speaking; especially if you've had a bit of a walk or gone up steps to a platform. This will give your voice a chance to adjust and be normal in a 'nervous' situation.
- Breathing is the most important point in being a good speaker. Breathe from your diaphragm, deeply and fully. Vocal sounds are made when air passes across your larynx. If you aren't breathing properly, your ability to project is diminished.

- Check out the room and sound system before you speak.
- Try speaking in the spot where you'll be presenting to allow yourself to become acclimatized to the environment and to reduce your nervousness. Have the soundman adjust for your range — from soft to the highest volume so you'll be comfortable and still be heard.
- Don't smoke or drink coffee or caffeine-based products before you speak. The caffeine can act as a diuretic, putting pressure on your bladder when you really don't need it. Smoking will add hoarseness to your voice and minimize the fluid in your mouth. This can minimize your ability to fully speak and project warmth and friendliness.

Remember your voice box is a muscle. It works better when warmed up and taken care of prior to speaking.

There may be no single thing more important in our efforts to achieve meaningful work and fulfilling relationships than to learn to practice the art of communication.
Max De Pree

Public Speaking Tips
A quick review

Here are a few reminders for your use:

- **Eye contact:** Look at the audience and make sure you pause long enough to make eye contact with specific people in various parts of the audience. Finish a thought and move on to the next person.
- **Gestures:** Select and use gestures that reinforce or illustrate what you are saying. Make sure they are consistent with what you are saying, or they will kill you on the platform.
- **Enthusiasm:** To be enthusiastic – act enthusiastic! If you don't believe it, why should your audience? And if they don't believe it, they won't buy it!
- **Articulation:** Make sure you pronounce the words carefully to enhance your audience's understanding. If they don't hear you clearly, they will misunderstand what you are saying.
  With over 5000 meanings based on the connotation for about 500 more commonly used business words, this is critical. More so, since we have people in our audiences for which English is a second language.
- **Breathe:** Make sure you breathe and allow the richness of your voice, your tone, and your delivery add value and meaning to your words.
- **Posture:** Stand tall and speak confidently when you address an audience. This stance adds credibility and believability to your words.
- **Tone:** Make sure your tone reflects and reinforces your words and your intent.
- **Dress:** As said, dress for success – not excess! Show respect and dress accordingly.

- **Language:** Keep it simple, relevant and cut out the $25-dollar words. You don't impress me, but you might distract me from what you are saying.
- **Smile:** When you've done your homework and are ready and relaxed, let your smile out – a lot!

What audiences know... without being told

...how you feel that day

...if you **don't** like or respect them

...when you've memorized your presentation

...when you're lying or bluffing

...when you're giving them a sales pitch

...when you've given up on yourself

Never underestimate the sensitivity of your audience! They are subconsciously aware of more than you realize. Be open and let them in!

A final word:

"To speak much is one thing, to speak well, another." **Sophocles**

I trust the tips shared in **Pocket Wisdom for Speakers** will assist you in your quest to be a more effective presenter. Being a better communicator is a positive career move. It is also a tool to help you work better with teams and perhaps even propel you into a leadership role.

This ongoing quest will push you into a lifetime of learning.

I joined Toastmasters to work on my speaking 28 years ago. I've spent 25 of those in a highly paid professional capacity and I am still learning. And, I love it!

We can only cover a few basics in this little publication. When I was teaching at college, I spent 35 hours with my students working through these techniques and much more. I challenged them to join a Toastmasters club to continue working honing their speaking skills. Putting these tips into practice is what works! I'd suggest that to you for that same reason. **www.Toastmasters.org**

They work, when you do!

Copyright and license notes

'Pocket Wisdom for Speakers (Updated 3rd edition)
How to captivate and connect with your audience

Bob 'Idea Man' Hooey, Accredited Speaker, 2011 Spirit of CAPS recipient. Prolific author of 30 plus business, leadership, and career success publications

Photos of Bob: **Dov Friedman**, www.photographybyDov.com
Bonnie-Jean McAllister, www.elantraphotography.com
Frédéric Bélot, www.fredericbelot.fr/fr
Trevor Schneider, www.interiorphotos.ca
Editorial, layout and design: **Irene Gaudet,** Vitrak Creative Services (a division of Creativity Corner Inc.), vitrakcreative.com

ISBN 13: 9781793820464

Printed in the United States 10 9 8 7 6 5 4 3 2 1
Success Publications – a division of Creativity Corner Inc.
Box 10, Egremont, AB T0A 0Z0
www.successpublications.ca
Creative office: 1-780-736-0009

Acknowledgements, credits, and disclaimers

As with each of my books, a very special dedication of this piece of myself, to the two people who meant the most to me, my folks **Ron and Marge Hooey**. Sadly, both my parents left this earthly realm in 1999. I still miss our time together and your encouragement and love. I was blessed with the two of you in my life. I've added **George and Lillian Sidor** (Irene's folks) to this gratitude list.

To my inspiring wife and professional proof reader and publications coach, **Irene Gaudet**, who loves, encourages, and supports me in my quest to continue sharing my **Ideas At Work!** across the world. Thank you seems so inadequate for your timely work in helping make my writing and my client service better! I love the time we spend together!

To my colleagues and friends in the National Speakers Association (NSA), the Canadian Association of Professional Speakers (CAPS), and the Global Speakers Federation (GSF) who continually challenge me to strive for success and increased excellence.

To my great audiences, leaders, students, coaching clients, and readers across the globe who share their experiences and enjoyment of my work. Your positive and supportive feedback encourages me to keep working on additional programs and success publications like this updated version. My experience with you creates the foundation for additional real-life experiences I can take from the stage to the page, the classroom to the boardroom.

My thanks to a select few friends for your ongoing support and 'constructive' abuse. You know who you are. ☺

Disclaimer

We have not attempted to cite all the authorities and sources consulted in the preparation of this book. To do so would require much more space than is available. The list would include departments of various governments, libraries, industrial institutions, periodicals, and many individuals. Inspiration was drawn from many sources, including other books by the author; in this updated creation of Pocket Wisdom for Speakers

This book is written and designed to provide information on more effective use of your time, as a life and leadership enhancement guide. It is sold with the 'explicit' understanding that the publisher and/or the author are not engaged in rendering legal, accounting, or other Professional services. If legal or other expert assistance is required, the services of a competent Professional in your geographic area should be sought.

It is not the purpose of this book to reprint all the information that is otherwise available. Its primary purpose is to complement, amplify, and supplement other books and reference materials already available. You are encouraged to search out and study all the available material, learn as much as possible, and tailor the information to your individual needs. This will help to enhance your success in being a more effective sales person, leader or professional.

Every effort has been made to make this book as complete and as accurate as possible within the scope of its focus. However, there may be mistakes, both typographical and in content or attribution. Graphics are royalty free or under license. Care has been taken to trace ownership of copyright material contained in this volume. The publisher will gladly receive information that will allow him to rectify any reference or credit line in subsequent editions. This book should be used only as a general guide and not as the ultimate source of information. Furthermore, this book contains information that is current only up to the date of publication.

The purpose Pocket Wisdom for Speakers' is to educate and entertain; perhaps to inform and to inspire. It is certainly to challenge its readers to learn and apply its secrets and tips, to challenge them to enhance their skills and leverage their time to create more Productive outcomes. The author and publisher shall have neither liability nor responsibility to any person or entity with respect to any loss or damage caused, or alleged to have been caused, directly or indirectly, by the information contained in this book.

Bob's B.E.S.T. publications

Bob is a prolific author who has been capturing and sharing his wisdom and experience in print and electronic formats for the past fifteen plus years. In addition to the following publications, several of them best sellers, he has written for consumer, corporate, professional associations, trade, and on-line publications. He has been engaged to write and assist on publications by other best-selling writers and successful companies. His publications are listed below.

Bob's Business Enhancement Success Tools

Leadership, business, and career success series
Running TOO Fast (8th edition 2018)
Legacy of Leadership (3rd edition 2016)
Make ME Feel Special! (6th edition 2016)
Why Didn't I 'THINK' of That? (5th edition 2015)
Speaking for Success! (8th edition 2016)
THINK Beyond the First Sale (3rd edition 2017)
Prepare Yourself to WIN! (3rd edition 2018)

Bob's mini-book success series
The Courage to Lead! (4th edition 2017)
Creative Conflict (3rd edition 2017)
Get to YES! (3rd edition 2017)
THINK Before You Ink! (3rd edition 2017)

Running to Win! (2nd edition 2017)
How to Generate More Sales (4th edition 2017)
Unleash your Business Potential (3rd edition 2017)
Learn to Listen (2nd edition 2017)
Creativity Counts! (3rd edition 2016)
Create Your Future! (3rd edition 2017)

Co-authored books created by Bob
Quantum Success – 3 volume series (2006)
In the Company of Leaders (3rd edition 2014)
Foundational Success (2nd edition 2013)

Bob's Pocket Wisdom series: *(coming as e-books in 2019)*
Pocket Wisdom for **Selling Professionals** (updated 2019)
Pocket Wisdom for **Speakers** (updated 2019)
Pocket Wisdom for **Innovators**
Pocket Wisdom for **Leaders – Power of One!** (updated 2019)
Pocket Wisdom for **Business Builders**

Bob's Idea-rich leaders edge series: *(new 2018-2019)*
LEAD! 12 idea-rich leadership success strategies
CREATE! Idea-rich strategies for enhanced innovation
TIME! Idea-rich tips for enhanced performance and productivity
SERVE! Idea-rich strategies for enhanced customer service
SPEAK! Idea-rich tips and techniques for great presentations
CREATIVE CONFLICT Idea-rich leadership for team success
SELL! Idea-rich techniques for sales success

Visit: www.SuccessPublications.ca for more information on Bob's publications and other success resources.

Email: bob@ideaman.net or visit:
www.SuccessPublications.ca

What they say about Bob 'Idea Man' Hooey

 As I travel across North America, and more recently around the globe, sharing my Ideas At Work!, I am fortunate to get feedback and comments from my audiences and colleagues. These comments come from people who have been touched, challenged, or simply enjoyed themselves in one of my sessions. **I'd love to come and share some ideas with your organization and teams.**

"I still get comments from people about your presentation. Only a few speakers have left an impression that lasts that long. You hit a spot with the tourism people." **Janet Bell**, Yukon Economic Forums

"Thank you, Bob, it is always a pleasure to see a true professional at work. You have made the name 'Speaker' stand out as a truism - someone who encourages people to examine their lives and adjust. The personal stories you shared with your audience made such a great impression on everyone. The comments indicated you hit people right where it is important - in their hearts. Each of those in your audience took away a new feeling of personal success and encouragement." **Sherry Knight**, Dimension Eleven Human Resources and Communications

"I am pleased to recommend Bob 'Idea Man' Hooey to any organization looking for a charismatic, confident speaker and seminar leader. I have seen Bob in action on several occasions, and he is ALWAYS on! Bob has the ability to grab his audience's attention and keep it. Quite simply, if Bob is involved - your program or seminar is guaranteed to succeed." **Maurice Laving**, Coordinator Training and Development, London Drugs

*"On very short notice Bob cleared his schedule and graciously presented at our meeting when the original Speaker was unable to attend. **Last week Bob set the tone for our two-day leadership meeting and gave us all a motivational lift.** His compassion and true interest in people was clearly evident, making him very credible. He shared some great stories, has a wealth of experience and knowledge and it was a pleasure listening to him. His down-to-Earth style makes it easier to retain the information presented. He also followed up with additional info and handouts, cementing his message of building bridges, not walls. Fantastic job, Bob, and thanks again!"*
Barbara Afra Beler, MBA, Senior Specialist Commercial Community, Alberta North, **BMO Bank of Montreal**

*"**I have been so excited working with Bob Hooey**, as he has given inspiration and motivation to our leadership team members. Both at the Brick Warehouse – Alberta and at Art Van Furniture – Michigan; with his years of experience in working with business executives and his humorous and delightful packaging of his material, he makes learning with Bob a real joy. But most importantly, anyone who encounters his material is the better for it."* **Kim Yost**, former CEO Art Van Furniture, former CEO The Brick

Motivate your teams, your employees, and your leaders to 'productively' grow and 'profitably' succeed!

Protect your conference investment - leverage your training dollars.

Enhance your professional career and sell more products and services.

Equip and motivate your leaders and their teams to grow and succeed, 'even' in tough times!

Leverage your time to enhance your skills, equip your teams, and better serve your clients.

Leverage your leadership and investment of time to leave a significant legacy!

Call today to engage best-selling author, award winning, inspirational leadership keynote speaker, leaders' success coach, and employee development trainer, **Bob 'Idea Man' Hooey** and his innovative, audience based, results-focused, **Ideas At Work!** for your next company, convention, leadership, staff, training, or association event. You'll be glad you did!

Call 1-780-736-0009 to connect with Bob 'Idea Man' Hooey today!
www.ideaman.net or
www.BobHooey.training

Thanks for reading Pocket Wisdom for Speakers

Each time I prepare to step on the stage; each time I sit down to write, or in this case to re-write, I am challenged to ensure I deliver something that will be of **use-it-now value** to my reader.

I ask myself, "If I was reading this, what would I be looking for?"

As well as, "Why is this relevant to me, today?"

These two questions help to keep me focused and help me to remain clear on my objectives. They help to remind me to dig into my experiences, stories, examples, and research to provide solid information that will be of benefit and help my readers, when they apply it, succeed. That can be an exciting challenge!

I trust I have done that for you in this updated primer. ***Pocket Wisdom for Speakers*** is my attempt to capture some of the lessons learned *first-hand* serving on various teams and in leadership roles and to share them with you. We need more leaders, now, more than ever. The world is crying out for more compassionate and courageous leaders. I hope you will step up and step into your role as a more effective and influential leader.

I'd love to hear from you and read your success stories. If you would be so kind, please drop me a quick email at:
bob@ideaman.net

Bob 'Idea Man' Hooey
2011 Spirit of CAPS recipient
www.ideaman.net
www.BobHooey.training

Bob speaking in Mumbai, India

www.ingramcontent.com/pod-product-compliance
Lightning Source LLC
Chambersburg PA
CBHW071158220526
45468CB00003B/1065